MW00849625

Boston Terrier Training Triumphs

A Guide to Raising the Perfect Pup

by Lacy Peters

Copyright 2023 Archieboy Holdings, LLC.
All rights reserved.

Formatted, Converted, and Distributed by eBookIt.com
http://www.eBookIt.com

ISBN-13: 978-1-4566-4083-5 (paperback)
ISBN-13: 978-1-4566-4084-2 (ebook)
ISBN-13: 978-1-4566-4085-9 (audiobook)

No part of this book may be reproduced in any form or
by any electronic or mechanical means including
information storage and retrieval systems, without
permission in writing from the author. The only
exception is by a reviewer, who may quote short excerpts
in a review.

Table of Contents

Introduction

Oh, hello there! You've just brought home a bundle of joy with a heart-shaped nose, or perhaps you're about to. Congratulations, you've selected or are considering one of the most charming, intelligent, and downright hilarious breeds out there - the Boston Terrier. Nicknamed the "American Gentleman," this breed is as sophisticated as they come, with their tuxedo-like markings and refined demeanor. But don't let that fool you; they've got an uncanny sense of humor that'll have you laughing out loud on the daily.

Let me introduce myself. I'm a lifelong Boston Terrier enthusiast, much like yourself, or at least, like the person you're about to become. I've spent the majority of my life walking, talking, and occasionally, if I'm honest, bargaining with these delightful creatures. They're a breed like no other, and with their winning personalities and human-like quirks, they can turn even the sternest of hearts into marshmallows.

When it comes to the Boston Terrier breed, they say every dog has its day. But with a

Boston Terrier, it's more like every day is a dog's day. Their liveliness, charm, and extreme friendliness make them the life of any party. However, as with all breeds, there are unique aspects to their temperament and behavior that new owners should understand to ensure that every day is a good dog day.

Our journey through this book is going to be as unpredictable, fun-filled, and satisfying as the breed itself. We'll start by exploring the roots of the Boston Terrier, which are as intriguing as those stories your grandpa used to tell about his world travels. Yes, the ones that began with "Did I ever tell you about the time..."

From there, we'll dive into understanding what makes a Boston Terrier tick. Much like your favorite rom-com, Boston Terriers are full of surprises. They can be stubborn and independent but also sweet and eager to please. There's a reason they're often considered the comedians of the dog world. In short, knowing a Boston is like keeping up with a riveting Netflix series. And much like the binge-worthy sensation, they'll keep you captivated, episode after episode, or in this case, tail wag after tail wag.

We'll then transition into the fascinating world of training your Boston Terrier. As a pet parent, you'll wear many hats – coach, mentor, BFF, food provider – the list goes on. But one of the most crucial roles you'll play is that of a teacher. Whether it's house training, teaching basic commands, or tackling more advanced tricks, we'll be right there with you, cheering you on and providing the guidance you need.

Just when you think you've learned all there is to know about your dapper little friend, we'll venture into the world of socialization. Boston Terriers are known to be quite the social butterflies, but like any butterfly, they need a little help coming out of their cocoon. You'll learn how to create a social superstar, making friends at dog parks and Instagram dog influencers in no time.

Of course, a happy Boston Terrier doesn't just require great training and socialization. They also need the right nutrition and exercise to keep their tail wagging and those big, round eyes sparkling. We'll dig into the essentials of feeding your Boston Terrier, from puppyhood to senior years. As they say, "You are what you eat," and this applies to our furry friends as well.

Lastly, we'll face some of the inevitable challenges that come with raising a Boston Terrier. Even the most perfect pup can have behavioral issues or grow old. But don't worry, we've got you covered. We'll discuss how to tackle common behavioral problems and how to cater to the needs of an aging Boston.

Whether you're already head over heels for your Boston Terrier or are just starting to feel those puppy-love butterflies, you're in for a treat. This guide is the ultimate joyride through Boston Terrier ownership, peppered with the right amount of humor, expert tips, and heart-warming moments. Ready? Let's embark on this exciting journey together!

The Pint-Sized Patriot - A History of Boston Terriers

Just imagine Boston in the 1870s. Cobblestone streets, horse-drawn carriages, and top hats were the latest trend, and right in the middle of it all, a strapping chap by the name of Robert C. Hooper made an investment that would rewrite canine history. Picture this - he brought home a sturdy, somewhat dashing dog named Judge. It was the kind of decision that seemed just a smidge impulsive, like splurging on a pair of Gucci sneakers you absolutely don't need but suddenly can't live without.

Judge, our four-legged protagonist, was a Bull and Terrier mix, the doggy lovechild of an

English Bulldog and a White English Terrier. He had the strength of a bulldog and the energy of a terrier, essentially the Victorian equivalent of a Red Bull can with legs. But what made Judge truly noteworthy was his lineage. You see, this pup wasn't just any dog; he was the Adam of all Boston Terriers.

So, Mr. Hooper did what any reasonable dog owner with a one-of-a-kind canine would do - he set up Judge with the most eligible bachelorette on the block, a petite white damsel known only as Burnett's Gyp or Kate. Now, Kate was no ordinary pup either. Half the size of Judge, with a gentle demeanor and a fur as white as a Boston winter, she was the yin to Judge's yang. Their first date was most likely an elegant affair, and if dog dates were a thing back then, they'd probably involve some choice cuts of steak and a moonlit walk in the park.

From this powerful union, came one puppy, a male who combined the best of both his parents. And just like that, in the heart of Boston, the first generation of the Boston Terrier breed was born. This puppy was bred with a French Bulldog, and thus began the lineage that led to our modern Boston Terriers. I can almost hear the "awws" resonating.

Fast forward a few decades, and this new breed was making waves in the dog world. Their friendly disposition, combined with a compact size and a dapper tuxedo-like coat, made them the perfect pet for city-dwelling folks. And trust me, nothing says "city chic" like a little dog that looks like it's perpetually dressed for the Met Gala.

By 1891, the breed had won over so many hearts that the American Kennel Club couldn't ignore them. The Boston Terrier was officially recognized as a breed. But it didn't stop there. Oh, no! By 1915, the Boston Terrier was one of the most popular breeds in the United States. That's like going from being a new kid in school to the prom king in just two decades.

The Boston Terrier's star continued to rise through the 20th century, featuring in ads, TV shows, and even serving as mascots for universities. It's like they were born for the limelight. A Boston Terrier named Rhett serves as Boston University's live mascot, and I don't know about you, but a doggy mascot sounds way more appealing than a human in a foam costume.

Today, the Boston Terrier is as American as apple pie and baseball. These dapper little dogs have trotted their way into our homes and hearts with their tuxedo-like coats, expressive eyes, and perky ears. Plus, their sociable and friendly nature, along with their adaptability to apartment living, make them a popular choice for urbanites and families alike.

So there you have it, the humble (yet thoroughly charming) history of Boston Terriers. From the cobblestone streets of 1870s Boston to the cozy city apartments of the 21st century, these compact canines have truly earned their place as the American Gentleman of the dog world. And to think, all this started with an impulsive decision by a certain Mr. Hooper. Here's to life's unexpected surprises, especially when they come with four legs and a tail.

The Boston Unpacked - Understanding Your Boston Terrier

So, you're considering bringing a Boston Terrier into your life, or you've already taken the leap. That's like deciding to add a little black dress to your wardrobe. It's classic, it's chic, and it's a decision you'll never regret.

First off, let's talk looks. Boston Terriers are, hands down, one of the most stylish breeds out there. They're born in a tuxedo, after all! Compact and muscular, they carry a certain elegance with their square proportions and distinct markings. And those expressive eyes? They're the ultimate window to your pooch's soul - and are also highly adept at demanding treats. Resistance is futile!

Next, their personality. Boston Terriers are an amazing cocktail of joy, mischief, and absolute loyalty. They're friendly, bright, and oh-so adaptable. They'll just as happily lounge on your couch during a Netflix marathon as they will play fetch in the park. These dogs are the ultimate social butterflies, ensuring you'll never have a dull moment, whether it's getting dragged into playtime at the crack of dawn or finding your shoe collection turned into a chew toy buffet.

Now, let's get into their intelligence. These dogs are sharp, like 'solve a Rubik's cube while doing a handstand' sharp. They're easy to train and love learning new tricks. You'll be showing off their high-five skills to your friends in no time. Just remember, with great intelligence comes great responsibility. You're going to want to keep that clever brain stimulated. So, stock up on puzzle toys, and brace yourself for rounds of hide-and-seek!

Speaking of energy, Boston Terriers pack quite the punch. They're a brachycephalic breed, which is just a fancy way of saying they've got a short nose and a flat face. While this gives them their distinct adorable look, it also means they can struggle with heat and strenuous exercise. It's like they're perpetually dressed for a winter in Boston even in the heat of summer. So, remember to pace their playtime and always have water handy.

When it comes to grooming, Boston Terriers are about as low-maintenance as a succulent. Their short, smooth coat is easy to manage, and they don't shed much. They're not hypoallergenic, but they're as close as you can get without landing in the realm of poodles or hairless cats. So, kiss goodbye to spending hours vacuuming dog hair off your couch!

At the risk of sounding like a cheesy dating profile, Boston Terriers also love long walks. They don't need hours of running like some breeds, but a nice, leisurely stroll keeps them fit and happy. Just remember, they are the embodiment of the saying, "It's not about the destination; it's about the journey." Be prepared for lots of stops and sniffs!

Now, onto communication. Boston Terriers might not have the vocal range of Mariah Carey, but they're not mute either. They have a variety of sounds to express their feelings, from happy yips to grumpy grumbles, and it's all part of their charm. They also have a master's degree in non-verbal communication. A tilt of the head, a wag of the tail, or a long, meaningful stare can speak volumes.

Nutrition is another key area for these little dynamos. Boston Terriers can be a bit on the greedy side and prone to obesity if overfed. It's important to measure their meals and limit treats. Keep them lean and mean – well, not mean, these little guys wouldn't hurt a fly unless it's encased in a chew toy!

In conclusion, understanding your Boston Terrier is like getting to know a new best friend. They're full of quirks and charms, and while they might not be perfect (who is?), they're perfectly wonderful in their own unique way. So, here's to navigating this fabulous journey together, filled with slobbery kisses, wagging tails, and memories to last a lifetime.

Chapter 1: Setting the Stage for Success

Welcome to the wonderfully whimsical world of Boston Terriers, where life is never dull, and your footwear is never safe! In this thrilling dog-adventure you're about to embark on, success lies in preparation - sort of like prepping for a dinner party, but with fewer canapes and more chew toys. It's all about understanding your dog, creating a comfy environment, maintaining a balanced diet (no, not yours, the dog's), ensuring regular exercise, and communicating effectively. It's about finding that sweet spot between being the chilled-out buddy and the disciplined pack leader. Think of it like being a mix of Oprah and a seasoned army sergeant. But worry not, this guide will help you navigate this journey like a pro, ensuring you and your new tuxedo-clad furball (or potential furball) share a lifetime of love, joy, and never-ending entertainment. Let's do this!

Teaching Your Pooch to Vogue - The Basics of Training

So, you've got your Boston Terrier, your new best friend, your confidante, your partner in crime (note: this is a metaphor; please refrain from actual crime). Now, the next step is training your four-legged companion, which is much like teaching a toddler or training a Kardashian to stay away from the limelight - full of ups, downs, and a whole lot of laughs.

First up, timing is everything. Start training your Boston Terrier as soon as they settle into your home. It's like hitting the gym in January - there's no better time to start than now. Puppies have an insatiable curiosity and a mind that absorbs things faster than a Gen-Zer scrolling through TikTok.

Next, let's talk training methods. Positive reinforcement is your best friend here. Much like us, Boston Terriers respond better to praise than to criticism. The principle is simple: reward the behaviors you like, and ignore the ones you don't. Yes, it's like selectively liking posts on Instagram, but with more puppy eyes and less screen time.

Treats are the currency of the dog world and a powerful tool in your training arsenal. But remember, Boston Terriers can be little foodie fiends and have a propensity to overindulge. So, be mindful of the size and healthiness of the treats you're using. Choose small, low-calorie options or pieces of fruits and veggies. Let's aim for more Kendall Jenner, less cookie monster.

When it comes to training sessions, short and sweet is the mantra. Boston Terriers, while intelligent, have a relatively short attention span. It's like trying to keep a kid interested in homework while their favorite cartoon is on. Aim for 5-10 minute sessions, a few times a day. Anything longer and you're likely to lose your dog's focus faster than a trend fades on Twitter.

Consistency is key in training. If you're training your dog not to jump on the couch, everyone in the family needs to follow suit. Mixed messages can be confusing, and before you know it, your Boston Terrier will be lounging on the sofa, wearing your favorite hat, and flipping channels with the remote.

Socialization is another crucial aspect of your Boston Terrier's training. Expose them to different environments, people, and other pets. It's like broadening their social network, only more fun and less prone to misinformation.

Properly socialized dogs are happier and easier to handle. So, take them out on puppy dates, to the park, or just a stroll around the block.

Training isn't just about commands and tricks. It also involves house-training, which, let's face it, can sometimes feel like an uphill battle. Patience and a regular schedule can do wonders here. And always remember, accidents happen. So don't lose your cool if you step into a surprise puddle. It's all part of the process.

Let's not forget the importance of training your pooch to walk nicely on a leash. Boston Terriers can be a bit excitable and may turn into mini freight trains if they spot a squirrel or another dog. Regular practice, coupled with positive reinforcement, can help your pup become a model leash-walker, making your daily walks a breeze.

Lastly, always end training sessions on a positive note. It's like finishing a workout with a good stretch, only fluffier. It helps ensure that your Boston Terrier associates training with happy memories and looks forward to the next session.

There you have it, the basics of training your Boston Terrier. Remember, every dog learns at their own pace, so don't be disheartened if progress seems slow. In the end, the bonding and mutual respect that develop through training are worth every moment. After all, a well-trained Boston Terrier isn't just a pet; they're the ultimate partner-in-crime (again, metaphorically!). Now, go have fun training your furball!

The Tool Belt for Canine Instruction - Tools and Resources for Training

Think of yourself as the MacGyver of dog training. You need a certain set of tools and resources to help you guide your Boston Terrier towards becoming the best they can be. It's less about defusing bombs and more about diffusing bad behavior, but the principle's the same!

First, let's talk leashes. Your leash is your lifeline to your dog, much like Wi-Fi is to your Netflix binge sessions. When it comes to training, a standard 6-foot leash is perfect. It's long enough to give your dog some freedom, but short enough for you to maintain control. Avoid retractable leashes during training, they're like giving a toddler a permanent marker - it'll probably end in chaos.

Now, onto the collar. A flat collar with a secure buckle is ideal for most Boston Terriers. It's simple, effective, and won't get in the way of their natural suaveness. If you're facing persistent pulling problems, a no-pull harness might be a good investment. It's like power steering for your dog, giving you better control without causing discomfort.

Training treats are your secret weapon. Remember how we talked about using positive reinforcement for training? Well, treats are your best reinforcement allies. Pick small, tasty morsels that your dog loves but won't pile on the pounds.

Next up are toys. Interactive toys, like puzzle feeders or Kongs, can be a fantastic resource for keeping your Boston Terrier's clever brain engaged. These toys are like Sudoku for your dog - challenging, stimulating, and a great boredom buster.

A clicker can be a nifty tool in your training arsenal. It makes a distinctive sound that tells your dog, "Good job, buddy! Treat's coming!" It's like sending a text with a guaranteed immediate response. Just remember, consistency is crucial. The click must always be followed by a reward.

Training pads can be a godsend during the house-training phase. They're absorbent, easy to clean, and help contain those inevitable accidents. Think of them as the diaper of the dog world, just a lot less... well, you know.

A crate can be an invaluable tool, especially during the early stages of training. When used correctly, it can be a safe haven for your dog and aid in house-training. It's their own personal studio apartment, right in the heart of your home!

Don't forget the value of professional help. Dog trainers and obedience classes can offer valuable insights and guidance, especially if you're new to this. It's like hiring a personal trainer at the gym - sometimes, having a pro can really amp up your results.

Online resources like YouTube tutorials, dog training blogs, and online forums can also provide a wealth of information. It's like having a virtual dog whisperer right at your fingertips.

Finally, remember that one of the most powerful tools in your training kit is patience. Training a Boston Terrier, or any dog, for that matter, takes time, persistence, and a whole lot of love. After all, Rome wasn't built in a day, and neither is a well-behaved Boston Terrier. But with these tools and resources at your disposal, you're well-equipped for the journey ahead. So gear up, and happy training!

Constructing Canine Nirvana - Creating a Positive Training Environment

Picture this: you're walking into a yoga studio, you've got the incense, the calming music, the soft lighting. It's tranquil, peaceful, a little slice of Zen. Now, I want you to imagine creating something similar for your Boston Terrier. No, not a yoga studio (though that would be adorable), but a positive training environment. It's all about setting the stage for success, tail-wagging style.

Firstly, remember that your Boston Terrier is a smart cookie. They're part of a breed that thrives on mental stimulation. So, your training environment should be a place that encourages learning and curiosity. Think of it as a doggie Montessori of sorts.

When you're training, minimize distractions. It's like studying for an exam. You wouldn't do it at a rock concert (unless you're into that kind of challenge). So, start training in a quiet room, away from the chaos of daily life. Once your pup's a pro, you can add in distractions bit by bit.

Positive reinforcement is, you guessed it, super important in setting the right atmosphere for training. Always reward good behavior. Praise, treats, belly rubs - your dog should associate training with all things good. It's like getting a gold star in school, only furrier.

Now, let's talk space. Your training environment should have enough room for your dog to move around freely. It's like needing floor space for a good TikTok dance-off. But in this case, it's for executing commands like 'sit', 'stay', and 'do the hustle'. Okay, maybe not the last one.

Consistency is key. Try to train in the same general area each time. This familiarity helps your Boston Terrier understand that it's 'learning time'. It's kind of like having a dedicated desk for work or study, but with more sniffing.

Remember, dogs, like humans, learn better when they're relaxed. So ensure your Boston Terrier is calm before you start a training session. No one learns well when they're wound up tighter than a Jack-in-the-box.

Try to keep the mood light during training. If you're stressed or frustrated, your dog will pick up on it. Trust me, a tense dog trainer leads to a tense dog. So, take a deep breath, channel your inner Tina Fey, and keep it fun.

Don't forget, training shouldn't be an all-day affair. Short, frequent training sessions are more effective. It's like binge-watching your favorite series. You enjoy it more in shorter bursts, rather than a 12-hour marathon.

Music might help create a soothing environment for training. Yes, you heard it right, music! Just as some humans study better with soft music playing, some dogs train better with a bit of Mozart or Beyonce in the background. Try it, it might just do the trick for your musically-inclined mutt.

Finally, remember to keep your training environment safe. No sharp objects, no toxic plants, and absolutely no chocolate lying around. A safe dog is a happy dog, and a happy dog is a learning dog.

And there you have it! With these tips, you're ready to create a positive training environment that's the equivalent of a doggie Harvard. So, set the stage, grab those treats, and let the training magic begin!

Chapter 2: Understanding Boston Terrier Behavior

If the Boston Terrier were a guest at a cocktail party, they'd be the charismatic life of the party, cracking wise jokes while smoothly navigating the room. These social butterflies are whip-smart and often showcase a playful stubbornness. Their expressive eyes tell a thousand tales - from sheer joy to a plea for that last bit of your steak. They've got energy in abundance, but also enjoy a good snooze in a cozy corner. They're vocal without being yappy, with a rich repertoire of barks, whines, and even grumbles when they're being particularly playful. Their keen sensitivity to their owner's emotions makes them a furry barometer of feelings in your home. Never underestimate their culinary curiosity or their knack for sneakily exploring forbidden territories when you're not looking. All in all, the Boston Terrier is a versatile, adaptable breed, at home in both the city and the countryside, making them the perfect companion for almost any lifestyle.

Meet Your Furry Therapist - Boston Terrier Temperament

Imagine the perfect roommate. They're good-natured, friendly, a tad hilarious, and always ready to offer a comforting presence. This, dear dog lover, is not a dream, it's a Boston Terrier!

Firstly, Boston Terriers are the poster pups for friendliness. They're social creatures who thrive on companionship. Be it other dogs, cats, or humans, they're likely to extend a friendly paw. Think of them as the canine embodiment of the phrase, "make love, not war."

In terms of intelligence, they're the doggy equivalent of the kid who always gets picked first in the schoolyard for the quiz team. They're bright, quick to learn, and have a surprising knack for problem-solving. But remember, their sharp wits can sometimes lead to a bit of stubbornness, because hey, nobody likes a know-it-all!

Now, if there were a doggie Oscars for 'Best in Expressiveness', the Boston Terrier would be a perennial nominee. They're remarkably good at conveying their feelings through their expressive eyes and a range of vocalizations. An excited yelp, a comforting whimper, or a playful growl - it's all part of their rich emotional vocabulary.

Did someone say party? Because your Boston Terrier is ready! Known for their high energy levels, they're always game for a fun romp or an impromptu fetch session. But they're not energy junkies; they appreciate downtime and are more than content to curl up for a cozy nap beside you.

What sets Boston Terriers apart is their sensitivity. They're in tune with your emotions, almost like they have a built-in mood detection system. Had a rough day? Your Boston Terrier is there, ready to lend a comforting paw or a loving lick.

Boston Terriers have an adventurous palate. They're food motivated and not too fussy about what they eat. While this can make training a little easier, remember to keep a check on their diet to avoid overfeeding or indulgence in inappropriate foods.

Their playful and mischievous side is hard to miss. Boston Terriers love to explore and have a knack for getting into places they probably shouldn't. While this makes for some great 'caught in the act' photos, it also calls for you to ensure a safe environment for their explorations.

Boston Terriers are known for their adaptability. They're equally at home in a bustling city apartment or a quiet country house. As long as they have you by their side and their basic needs are met, they're content.

Above all, Boston Terriers are known for their gentle and loving disposition. They're not just pets; they're part of your family, offering an unwavering, unconditional love that's a beautiful thing to experience.

In summary, the Boston Terrier's temperament makes them a joy to have around. They're friendly, intelligent, expressive, energetic, sensitive, playful, adventurous, adaptable, and gentle. They're like the friend you want to have around - always up for fun, but also there for you when you need some comfort. They're not just dogs; they're a lifestyle. So, brace yourself for a whole lot of love, laughter, and occasional stubbornness. Life with a Boston Terrier is never boring!

Boston Terrier Playbook - Common Boston Terrier Behaviors

Behold, the Boston Terrier, a breed with such an eclectic mix of behaviors, they could easily pass for a character in a sitcom. But don't worry, even though they can be mischievous, their quirks only add to their charm. Let's dive in and dissect some of their most common behaviors.

You've got to start with the 'Head Tilt'. Yes, with capital letters. It's a Boston Terrier's signature move. They'll cock their heads to one side like they're trying to decipher your every word. While it's a heart-meltingly adorable sight, it's also a sign of their attentiveness. They're great listeners, even if they don't always follow through with the 'obeying' part.

On the topic of attentiveness, Boston Terriers have a knack for eye contact. Not just a passing glance, but a deep, soul-searching gaze that screams, "I see you, human!" This strong eye contact is a sign of their intelligence and their desire to communicate with you.

Let's not forget the 'Boston Booty Shake'. This is not to be mistaken with the twerk. When a Boston Terrier is happy or excited, their whole body wags along with their tail. They basically turn into a wriggling bundle of joy. And if that doesn't put a smile on your face, I don't know what will.

Another well-known Boston Terrier behavior is their snorting, snuffling, and occasional snoring. They are brachycephalic, meaning they have short noses and flat faces, which can lead to these endearing (or annoying, depends on how much you value silence) sounds. It's all part of their charm, really.

Who needs an alarm clock when you have a Boston Terrier? These dogs tend to be early risers, ready to start their day at the crack of dawn. Whether it's excitement for their breakfast or a refreshing morning walk, they're ready to seize the day, even when you might not be.

The Boston Terrier is also something of a lap dog. Yes, despite their energy, they love nothing more than curling up on your lap for a nap or just some good old TLC. It's their way of showing affection and trust. Plus, they're not too big, so they won't cut off your circulation like some other breeds.

Known for their playfulness, Boston Terriers are fond of interactive games. Fetch is an all-time favorite, but they're also quite adept at hide and seek. It's a fun way to stimulate their minds and satisfy their natural curiosity.

Boston Terriers often exhibit the 'Zoomies', sudden bursts of energy where they run around like they're competing in the Dog Olympics. Don't worry, they're not going mad. It's just a way for them to release excess energy and, let's be honest, it's pretty hilarious to watch.

As with any dog breed, Boston Terriers can exhibit resource guarding, a behavior where they protect their food, toys, or territory. While not unique to Boston Terriers, it's something to be mindful of. With proper training and socialization, this behavior can be managed.

Lastly, Boston Terriers are renowned for their 'Shadowing' behavior. They love being around their humans so much, they'll often follow you from room to room, keeping a watchful eye on your activities. It's a little like having a furry, four-legged stalker, but in a cute way.

So there you have it, the Boston Terrier in all their delightful, quirky glory. From the charming 'Head Tilt' to the adorable 'Boston Booty Shake', each of these behaviors paints a vivid picture of their unique personality. Life with a Boston Terrier is a roller-coaster of laughter, cuddles, and the occasional early morning wake-up call. But trust me, it's a ride worth taking!

All the Positive Vibes - Encouraging Positive Behavior

Boston Terriers are clever creatures with a dash of stubbornness thrown in for good measure. Now, before you panic, let's talk about how to channel that brainpower into positive behaviors. It's all about playing the right cards, setting clear boundaries, and, let's face it, a little bit of bribery.

First things first, reward good behavior. It sounds simple because it is. You know that proud feeling when your Boston Terrier actually listens and sits when told? Shower them with praises and maybe slip them a small treat. It's like adding a bonus point to their mental scoreboard. "Hmm, I sat, and I got a treat... Let's do that again!"

Training sessions should be a concoction of fun and structure. Bostons are quick learners, but they're not fans of monotony. Change things up to keep them engaged. It's kind of like their Netflix - they love new content, and they'll get bored if they have to repeat the same episode over and over.

Socialization is key. Get your Boston out and about, meeting new people and other dogs. This helps them become more comfortable in different environments and situations. It's like them having a social media account - they get to experience different things and meet a variety of people, but in real life.

Correcting bad behavior requires patience and consistency. Boston Terriers are smart, but they're not mind readers. If your Boston is barking incessantly, calmly tell them "Quiet", and when they do quiet down, reward them. It's the dog equivalent of "You scratch my back, I'll scratch yours."

A tired Boston is a good Boston. Regular exercise can do wonders for behavior. When they're worn out from a game of fetch or a brisk walk, they'll be too tired for mischief. Think of it as their version of gym time - it gets their energy out and leaves them feeling content.

Set clear boundaries. If you don't want them on the furniture, be firm but gentle in your training. A simple "Off" command can do wonders. However, this means ALL the furniture. Remember, they don't understand that your favorite armchair is off-limits but the old couch is fine. To them, it's all a potential nap spot.

Training tools can be a great help. From harnesses to clickers, there are tons of gadgets that can aid in positive behavior training. Just remember, the tool isn't the trainer, you are. These are just there to help you communicate effectively.

Boston Terriers thrive on routine. Consistent meal times, walks, and bedtimes can help keep your Boston feeling secure and well-behaved. It's like their personal planner - when they know what's coming next, they can relax and be their best selves.

Remember, every dog is unique, just like people. Some Boston Terriers might pick up on things quicker than others, and that's okay. The important thing is to be patient, consistent, and always keep things positive. After all, at the end of the day, they're not just Boston Terriers, they're part of the family.

And finally, give them love. Lots of it. Positive reinforcement isn't just about treats and praises. It's about making your Boston feel loved and secure. So, go on, shower them with belly rubs, play fetch until your arm aches, and give them all the cuddles. Because a loved Boston is a well-behaved Boston.

So grab that leash, stock up on those treats, and step into the exciting world of positive behavior training. Your Boston Terrier is ready to learn, and with you by their side, there's no limit to what they can achieve. Just remember, training isn't a chore - it's a journey of discovery, fun, and lots of wagging tails. So, let's get started, shall we?

Chapter 3: Basic Training Techniques - We're not just winging it!

Now, onto the nitty-gritty. Boston Terrier training doesn't require a PhD, but it does need some basics. Start with commands like "Sit," "Stay," "Down," and for the love of your favorite pair of shoes, "Leave it!" Be patient, clear, and consistent. And remember, a little positive reinforcement goes a long way. Picture your Boston Terrier like a tiny, furry, four-legged student, eager to learn but gets sidetracked by, well, everything! Keep your training sessions short, fun, and frequent. It's kind of like a super engaging TikTok video - short, impactful, and leaves them wanting more! Just remember, the goal isn't to create a robot dog, but to build a strong, loving bond with your cuddly sidekick.

Making Your House a Boston-Proof Zone - House Training 101

Welcome to the battlefield that is house training! But don't worry, it's not as scary as it sounds. With a game plan in hand and some Boston Terrier determination, your house will soon become their castle, minus the mess.

Let's start with the basics: Potty training. Choose a designated potty area outside and stick to it. Every time your Boston Terrier needs to go, lead them to this spot. It's like your Boston's very own VIP bathroom - exclusive and always open!

Keep a consistent feeding schedule. What goes in on a regular schedule will likely come out on a regular schedule. It's just basic doggy math. Plus, it gives you an idea of when your Boston might need to go potty, preventing those surprise 'gifts' on your carpet.

Be vigilant and observant. Puppies, especially, have a pretty predictable potty schedule. They'll need to go after they eat, play, or wake up from a nap. If you see them sniffing around or starting to squat, it's time for a quick trip to their designated potty area.

Accidents happen, so when they do, it's important to handle it right. Never punish your

Boston for having an accident. Instead, clean it up thoroughly with an enzyme-based cleaner to eliminate any lingering smells. It's like crime scene clean-up, Boston style!

Crate training can be a helpful tool when house training your Boston Terrier. It's not just a place for them to sleep, but it can also act as their personal space where they feel safe and secure. Think of it as their personal studio apartment within your house - cozy and all their own.

Chewing is another common hurdle in house training. If you find your Boston gnawing on something they shouldn't, like your favorite pair of shoes, replace it with a toy or chew that's theirs. Over time, they'll learn what's off-limits. It's the canine version of swapping a bad habit for a good one.

Jumping up can be a challenging behavior to curb, especially since your Boston Terrier is just so excited to see you. But remember, not everyone appreciates a doggy hello to the face. When they jump up, turn your back and ignore them. When all four paws are on the ground, that's when you give them attention. It's the Boston version of playing hard to get.

Barking can be another issue to address during house training. Teach your Boston the "Quiet" command, and always reward them when they get it right. And remember, some barking is okay. It's their way of communicating, after all. Just think of it as their little doggy language, and you're just trying to keep it on a 'library level.'

Patience is the name of the game when house training a Boston Terrier. There will be good days, and there will be 'Oh, crap!' days (quite literally). But remember, it's all a part of the journey. Think of it as an extended bonding activity - you're both learning about each other and figuring things out together.

At the end of the day, house training your Boston Terrier is about setting them up for success, and creating a happy, comfortable environment for both of you. So embrace the process, keep your sense of humor, and get ready for a wild and wonderful ride. After all, isn't that why we got ourselves into this doggy parent thing in the first place?

Taking the Lead - Leash and Walk Training

Leash training - it's like a dance between you and your Boston Terrier, where you're trying to lead, and they're... well, doing their own unique rendition of the Cha-Cha. But with patience, practice, and a dash of humor, your Boston will be strutting beside you like they're on a fashion runway.

The first step is choosing the right gear. Harnesses are a great option for Bostons, as they protect their small frames and delicate tracheas. When picking one out, imagine you're a personal stylist for your dog - it needs to be functional, comfortable, and of course, stylish.

Once you've got your gear, it's time for the first introduction. Let your Boston sniff and explore their new harness and leash. Treat it like a meet and greet - minus the awkward small talk. You can even let them wear it around the house to get used to the feel.

Start your leash training indoors where there are fewer distractions. Walk around your house with your Boston on the leash, luring them with treats and praise. It's a private fashion show, with treats as payment instead of applause.

Remember, Bostons are small dogs with big personalities. They might want to lead the way, but it's important for you to guide the pace and direction. So channel your inner strong, confident leader - you're not just a dog owner, you're a pack leader.

If your Boston pulls on the leash, stop walking. This teaches them that pulling won't get them where they want to go any faster. It's a bit like a game of red light, green light - only move forward when the leash is slack.

Gradually increase the level of distraction by practicing in different environments. Start in a quiet park before eventually moving onto busier streets. It's like level-upping in a video game, with each new environment posing a new challenge for your Boston.

When you're out and about, remember to bring along some small treats. Use them to reinforce good leash manners and distract your Boston from potential triggers, like squirrels or other dogs. It's a two-birds-one-stone solution - distraction and reward all in one!

Don't forget about the importance of regular breaks. Boston Terriers can get overheated easily, so it's essential to take regular water and rest breaks during your walks, especially on warmer days. Treat it like a mini picnic - just you, your Boston, and a water bottle instead of a basket.

Finally, remember that every dog learns at their own pace. Progress might be slow, and that's okay. The journey is just as important as the destination, so try to enjoy every step, misstep, and leap forward.

All in all, leash and walk training is all about patience, consistency, and understanding. And hey, the upside to all this training? You'll get a fit and happy Boston Terrier, and you might just clock in those 10,000 steps a day too!

Talk to the Paw - Basic Commands: Sit, Stay, and Come

In the world of dog training, "Sit", "Stay", and "Come" are like the Beatles of commands. They're timeless, universally recognized, and could be your ticket to harmony with your Boston Terrier. But how do we teach our Bostons these chart-topping hits? Well, get ready to tune in and turn it up because we're about to dive right into it.

First up on the playlist is "Sit". This one's like the pop song that's catchy and simple to remember. Start with your Boston Terrier standing in front of you. Hold a treat in your hand, and raise it above their head. As their nose points up to follow the treat, their butt should naturally go down. The moment it hits the floor, say "Sit" and reward them with the treat and praise. Repeat this until they start sitting when you give the command. With enough practice, your Boston will be hitting those "Sit" notes on cue.

Next up is the classic track, "Stay". This one requires a little more finesse and patience - it's like the ballad of dog training. Once your Boston has mastered the "Sit" command, you can introduce "Stay". Ask your Boston to sit, then hold out your hand in a 'stop' gesture and say "Stay". Take a step back, and if they stay in place, reward them. Gradually increase the distance and duration of the stay, always rewarding them for their patience and obedience. Remember, it's a slow song, so take your time with this one.

Finally, we have "Come", the anthem that could save your Boston from a potentially dangerous situation. It's the power ballad of dog training. With your Boston on a leash, squat down to their level and say "Come" in an enthusiastic tone while gently pulling on the leash. When they come to you, reward them with a treat and lots of praise. Like an encore performance, keep repeating this until they can do it without the guidance of the leash.

Between sessions, it's a good idea to have impromptu training moments throughout the day. Ask your Boston to "Sit" before you put their food bowl down, or have them "Stay" while you hide a toy for a fun game of fetch. These little rehearsals will help reinforce their training.

A great performer knows how to keep their audience engaged. Mix up the rewards you use to keep your Boston interested. Treats, praise, petting, or a favorite toy can all serve as motivation for your furry friend to hit those high notes.

It's also crucial to keep the training sessions short and sweet. Think of it like a radio hit - it's got to be catchy and concise. Bostons have a shorter attention span, so try to limit training to a few minutes at a time.

Timing is everything in music, and the same goes for dog training. Always reward your Boston immediately after they follow a command. It's like their applause, letting them know they've hit the right notes.

Like a good song, these commands will stick with your Boston over time. So, it's essential to keep them fresh with regular practice, like a band rehearsing before a big tour.

And remember, every dog has its own rhythm. Your Boston might pick up some commands quicker than others, and that's okay. The key is to keep it positive, patient, and always end on a high note.

So there you have it - the top three hits in the world of dog training. With a bit of practice and consistency, your Boston Terrier will be ready to take center stage and wow you with their performance!

Chapter 4: Advanced Training Techniques

Get ready for the fireworks as we step into the realm of advanced training techniques with your Boston Terrier. Imagine your little furball responding to commands like a soldier, but without the stern drill sergeant vibes. From "heel" (we're not talking about shoe parts here), "leave it" (a canine yoga for self-control), "place" (like the best seat in the house), to "sit pretty" (more of a doggie Pilates move), and even "high five" (because who doesn't love a paw-five from their best friend?). Let's not forget the ever-classic "roll over" and the dramatic "play dead". These aren't just tricks to show off at family gatherings (though they're great for that too), they're exercises that engage your Boston's mind, enhance your bond, and yes, give you some pretty awesome bragging rights. So, buckle up for this thrill ride as we transform your Boston Terrier from a basic command maestro to a virtuoso of canine choreography!

Teaching Your Boston Terrier to Fetch

Okay, get ready, because teaching your Boston Terrier to fetch is about to turn into one of those quirky TV sitcom episodes. Trust me, if it isn't already, the term "fetch" will become a part of your everyday vocabulary, and not just because of your ongoing "Mean Girls" references. You'll be saying it so much, you might even start dreaming about it! The good news? The process can be super fun, and nothing beats the joy on your Boston's face when they finally get the hang of it.

Before we dive into the actual training, let's address the elephant in the room. Yes, we're going to use treats. Lots of them. I mean, who can resist those pleading puppy eyes? But remember, moderation is key. After all, we're aiming for a fit and active Boston, not an overweight couch potato.

The first step in teaching your Boston to fetch is to get them interested in the object you want them to fetch. This could be a ball, a toy, a stick, or even that old sneaker they've been eyeing since you brought them home. Hold the object in your hand, let them sniff it, maybe give it a little squeeze or shake (the object, not the dog). Let them see that this object is fun and exciting. Who knows, you might find yourself getting excited about that old tennis ball too!

Once you have your Boston's undivided attention, it's time to introduce the concept of 'fetch'. Toss the object a short distance away and say "fetch" in an upbeat and encouraging tone. At first, they might just stare at you like you've lost your marbles. That's okay. Be patient, remember we're dealing with a Boston Terrier here, not a Border Collie.

If your Boston does run after the object, that's half the battle won. The challenge now is to get them to bring the object back to you. To coax them into doing this, you could run a few steps in the opposite direction, inviting them to chase you. It's a lot like playing hard to get, except with a furry little creature and a slobbery toy.

Now, getting them to actually drop the object once they've brought it back is another ball game altogether. If your Boston Terrier is anything like mine, they probably think this is now a game of keep-away. To overcome this, you could introduce a 'drop it' or 'leave it' command. Of course, this is easier said than done. It may take a few tries (or a lot) to get this right. But hey, Rome wasn't built in a day, and your Boston isn't going to become a fetch champ overnight.

Eventually, with consistent practice, your Boston will start to understand the concept of fetch. Once they've got the basics down, you can gradually increase the distance you throw the object, turning this into a great exercise for both of you. It's a win-win!

In conclusion, teaching your Boston Terrier to fetch may feel a bit like trying to ride a unicycle while juggling flaming torches at first. But trust me, it's all part of the fun. Remember, the aim of this exercise is not only to keep your Boston physically active but also to strengthen the bond between you two. And when they finally do fetch that ball and drop it at your feet, trust me, all the effort will be worth it. It's not just a game of fetch, it's a game of love. And you're both winning.

Remember, every Boston is unique. Your friend's Boston Terrier might fetch like a pro, while yours is more interested in chasing their tail or taking a nap. And that's okay! As long as you and your Boston are having fun and spending quality time together, you're doing it right. So, go on, enjoy this fetching journey, and don't forget to laugh along the way!

Teaching Your Boston Terrier to Rollover

Rolling over, it's not just for buttery croissants anymore! It's also one of the most endearing tricks you can teach your Boston Terrier. Not to mention, it's guaranteed to score them some extra belly rubs (and who doesn't love those?). So grab your doggo, a handful of treats, and let's get rolling...literally!

First things first. Before you get started, find a comfortable spot for your Boston Terrier to perform this trick. The living room carpet, a soft patch of grass, your bed (if you don't mind the extra dog hair), these are all good options. Hardwood or tiled floors? Not so much. Rolling over on a slippery surface is about as much fun as stepping on a Lego barefoot. Yikes!

Now that you've picked your spot, the next step is to get your Boston in a down position. For the lucky ones, your Boston might already be a pro at 'down'. For the rest of us, this might be the first real challenge. If your Boston looks at you with the "you want me to do what now?" expression, tempt them with a treat by moving it slowly from their nose towards their tail, guiding them into a down position.

Alright, so your Boston is now lying down. Hurray! Now what? Well, this is where the magic happens. Hold another treat close to your Boston's nose and slowly move it towards their shoulder. As they follow the treat, they should naturally roll over onto their back. If they do, give them the treat, and heaps of praise! If they don't, do not fear. This isn't an episode of 'Mission Impossible'. We'll get there!

Some Bostons might not roll over completely the first few times, and that's completely fine. It's like that yoga class you tried once; some moves take a bit of practice. Reward any effort towards the right movement. If they only roll onto their side, that's progress! Treat and praise them like they just won the doggy Olympics.

Once they've gotten the hang of rolling over, it's time to introduce the verbal cue. Say "rollover" as they start to make the motion, then reward them once they've completed the trick. Consistency is key here. Also, ensure your voice is as cheerful as a morning show host on coffee. Dogs respond well to positive, upbeat tones.

Now you may wonder, how many times should you practice this a day? A few short training sessions each day are more effective than one long one. Aim for about five minutes at a time, a few times a day. Remember, even Beyoncé needs breaks during her rehearsals.

The 'Rollover' trick is a fantastic way to engage your Boston Terrier's mind and body. Plus, it's a crowd-pleaser! Just imagine the next time you have friends over. "Oh this? Just a little something we've been working on," you'd say nonchalantly as your Boston perfectly performs a roll over. Cue the ooohs and aaahs!

However, always remember that each dog learns at their own pace. If your Boston Terrier masters 'rollover' in a day, that's fantastic! If they take a bit longer, that's perfectly fine too. The goal here is to have fun and enjoy the process. After all, training is as much about bonding with your dog as it is about teaching them new tricks.

To sum up, teaching your Boston Terrier to rollover is like teaching a toddler to do a somersault. It might take a little time, it might get a bit messy, but in the end, it's all worth it when you see them perform it with joy. Happy rolling, everyone!

Other Fun and Useful Tricks

Well, well, well. Aren't we feeling ambitious? You've mastered the basics, and now you're ready to up the ante in your dog trick portfolio.

Excellent! Buckle up because your Boston Terrier is about to become the life of the party.

Let's kick things off with "Sit Pretty." A.K.A., your Boston's future favorite trick to show off during family gatherings. Start by getting your Boston into a sit. Now hold a treat above their nose, high enough that they can't reach it but low enough to keep them interested. If they stand up, go back to the 'sit' and start over. Reward them when they lift their paws off the ground. Remember, don't rush things. This isn't a 100-meter sprint!

Next on our fabulous trick menu, the "High-Five." Every good party trick routine needs one, right? Begin in a sitting position. Hold a treat in your hand and close your fist around it. Raise your fist just out of your Boston's reach and say, "High Five." Your Boston will likely paw at your hand to get the treat. Open your hand, give them the treat, and act like they just won an Oscar.

Now let's get a bit dramatic with the trick known as "Play Dead." This one's for the thespians in the house! Ask your Boston to 'down.' Then show them a treat, saying "Bang" (or "Play Dead," depending on your dramatic preferences) and move the treat so that your Boston rolls onto their side. Give the treat as soon as they hit the ground. Who knew playing dead could be so lively?

Let's move on to the "Spin." Hold a treat at your Boston Terrier's nose level and slowly lead them in a circle. As soon as they complete the circle, say "Spin," give them the treat and get your cheerleader vibes on. If your Boston takes to this trick, you could teach them to spin in both directions!

Another fun and easy trick is "Take a Bow." Start when your Boston Terrier is standing. Hold a treat in front of their nose and slowly move it down and back between their front legs. As your Boston lowers their front end to follow the treat, say, "Take a Bow" and reward them. Ta-da! Your Boston Terrier is now ready for their Broadway debut.

Now, we understand that variety is the spice of life. So let's jazz things up with the "Wave" trick. Begin with the high-five command. Once your Boston lifts their paw for the high-five, pull your hand back just out of their reach. When they move their paw in the air, as if waving, reward them. And just like that, you have a Boston Terrier who can wave hello!

And if you're really looking to impress, there's the "Ring a Bell" trick. For this, you'll need a bell that your Boston can ring with their paw or nose. Place the bell near them and wait. The second they touch the bell, give them a treat. Soon they'll connect ringing the bell with getting a treat and you'll have a bell-ringing Boston! Imagine the possibilities!

As always, remember that patience is key in training. There might be moments of frustration, but there will be more moments of joy. There will be laughter (both at your Boston's antics and your own), and there will be bonding. So much bonding.

Practicing tricks helps not just in providing entertainment (although, let's be honest, that's a huge perk), but it also provides mental stimulation for your Boston Terrier and helps to deepen the bond between you. It gives your Boston Terrier an opportunity to engage their brains and use some of that Boston Terrier energy.

Also, when teaching these tricks, it's important to remember that every Boston Terrier is unique. They are not just "a Boston Terrier," but they are "YOUR Boston Terrier." They have their own personalities, strengths, and interests. What may work for one Boston might not work for another. So don't be afraid to modify these tricks to suit your Boston's personality and abilities.

Always keep training sessions fun and positive. A cheerful tone and lots of praise can go a long way. If your Boston isn't getting a trick, don't worry. Take a break and try again another time. And always end training sessions on a positive note, even if it's with a trick your Boston has known for years.

So, there you have it! A slew of new tricks to keep both you and your Boston Terrier entertained and mentally stimulated. Now go forth and make every day a little bit more 'pawsome'!

Chapter 5: Socializing Your Boston Terrier

In Chapter 5, we're going to dive into the social butterfly realm of the Boston Terrier world. We'll explore the importance of socialization for your little black and white friend, as well as tips and tricks to help them become the life of the doggy park. From introducing them to new friends of both the two-legged and four-legged variety, to ensuring they are comfortable in various environments, we'll cover it all. It's time to take off those training wheels and let your Boston Terrier experience all the wonderful, exciting, and tail-wagging aspects of the world around them. Let's create some adorable doggy friendships!

Why Socialization is Crucial

Picture this: You and your Boston Terrier - let's call him Captain Snuffles because that's honestly the most adorable name I could think of – are taking a leisurely stroll in the park. All of a sudden, a gigantic Golden Retriever bounds over, a twinkle in his eye and a wag in his tail. Now, the question is, does Captain

Snuffles stand his ground, or does he turn tail and run, tiny legs scrambling in the grass?

This scene brings us to a significant topic: socialization. Sure, Captain Snuffles looks charming with his perfectly symmetrical markings and that perky little tail, but he needs to be more than just a pretty face. He needs to be socially adept, too.

Why? Well, proper socialization helps dogs like Captain Snuffles handle new experiences, people, and animals with aplomb. Dogs who are well socialized are less likely to react out of fear or aggression to unfamiliar situations and creatures. Instead, they handle these scenarios with the grace of a seasoned diplomat at a state dinner.

Socialization is especially important for Boston Terriers due to their particular breed characteristics. Historically, Bostons were bred for companionship. These dogs are not solitary creatures – they thrive in company and crave interaction. In fact, they were bred to be the life of the party.

You see, Bostons are naturally sociable, and the lack of social interaction can lead to stress and anxiety. If they're not properly introduced to a variety of people, other dogs, and new environments early in life, they might develop behavioral issues. And trust me, no one wants a stressed-out dog. They don't just mope around; they turn into a whirling dervish of destructive energy.

And here's something else to consider: Boston Terriers are small but they pack a big personality in that compact frame. They're full of energy, and they need to channel that energy constructively. Without proper socialization, you could be looking at a scenario of, well, zoomies at midnight, constant barking at the mailman, or your precious shoes ending up as chew toys.

Socialization is also key to ensuring that your Boston Terrier plays well with other dogs. Because let's face it, you're not just raising a dog - you're raising a canine citizen. This means Captain Snuffles needs to be a dog's dog, not just a people's dog.

Getting your Boston used to other dogs helps them understand how to play properly without getting too rough or overly territorial. It's like teaching them the doggy equivalent of 'please' and 'thank you.'

Moreover, a properly socialized Boston Terrier is a pleasure to walk, to bring to dog parks, or even to dog-friendly coffee shops. They're comfortable in their skin (or should I say, fur?), they're confident, and they're well-mannered. It's like having a mini canine ambassador by your side, charming everyone they meet.

Plus, remember that Bostons are quite the smarty pants. They love to learn, explore, and understand the world around them. Proper socialization caters to this natural curiosity and provides them with constant mental stimulation.

And let's not forget, socialization is not just crucial for your dog, but also for you. A well-socialized dog is easier to handle, less likely to create awkward or dangerous situations, and generally, just more fun to be around. It's like the difference between having a wild house party where everything's out of control, or a well-organized get-together where everyone has a good time.

So, the bottom line is, socialization is crucial. It's not a mere luxury, but an essential part of raising a well-rounded Boston Terrier. It's an investment that pays off in the form of a happy, confident, and well-mannered pet.

Don't fret, we'll be taking a deep dive into how to get your Boston Terrier to be the belle or beau of the ball in the upcoming sections. In the meantime, Captain Snuffles eagerly awaits his chance to hobnob with the best of them. So, let's get him ready for the grand ball, shall we?

Strategies for Successful Socialization

Alright, we've established that socializing your Boston Terrier is crucial. Now let's dive into the "how." Think of this chapter as your Boston Terrier's little black book for becoming the most popular pup in town.

Start Early: The golden period for socializing puppies is between 3 and 16 weeks old. This is when puppies are most open to new experiences and least likely to be scared. So, it's time to roll out the red carpet and show your Boston the world. Just make sure they have had their vaccinations first. We want to expose them to the world, not expose them to diseases.

Variety is the Spice of Life: It's not enough to introduce your Boston to your Aunt Agnes and call it a day. They need to meet people of all shapes, sizes, ages, and colors. They should be familiar with men, women, children, and people in uniforms or those using mobility aids. Your Boston's social circle should look like a United Nations meeting, just with more fur.

Introduce Them to Other Pets: Of course, humans aren't the only creatures your Boston needs to get familiar with. Other dogs, cats, and even the occasional bunny or bird should be on their social list. Dog parks, friends with pets, or pet-friendly cafes can be great places for these introductions.

Harness the Power of Playdates: Yes, doggie playdates are a thing, and they're as adorable as they sound. Not only does your Boston Terrier get to make new friends, but they also learn important social skills, like not biting too hard or understanding when another dog doesn't want to play. Plus, they come back home tired, which means a quiet evening for you.

Expose them to Different Environments: Your Boston Terrier needs to be comfortable in a variety of situations. This includes loud, quiet, crowded, and empty spaces. This also includes various sights, sounds, and smells. Your Boston should be as comfortable at a bustling farmers market as they are in a quiet library.

Positive Reinforcement is Key: Remember, socialization should be a fun and positive experience for your Boston. So bring out the treats, the praises, and the belly rubs. If your Boston associates new experiences with good things, they'll be more eager to explore the world.

Use Training Classes: Puppy classes aren't just for learning how to sit and stay. They're also excellent opportunities for socialization. Your Boston will learn to focus on you, even when surrounded by other dogs and people, and they get to meet a bunch of new friends in a safe, controlled environment.

Keep it Chill: Remember that socialization isn't a one-time thing. It's not about cramming as many new experiences as possible in a short time. It's about steady, gradual exposure, so your Boston doesn't get overwhelmed. Slow and steady wins the race, or in this case, the adoration of the entire neighborhood.

Don't Force It: If your Boston seems scared or anxious, don't force them into the situation. Give them space and time to adjust. The last thing we want is for your Boston to associate new experiences with fear or stress.

Remember, it's okay if your Boston doesn't become a social butterfly overnight. It's a process. Some days, they might be more of a wallflower, and that's okay. What's important is that you're giving them the opportunity to experience the world in a safe, positive, and controlled manner.

So put on your best party hat, grab the treats, and get ready to introduce your Boston Terrier to the world. And remember, every pup's different. Your Boston might become a socialite, or they might prefer smaller gatherings. The important thing is that they're happy, confident, and not fearful of new experiences.

Chapter 6: Nutrition and Exercise for Your Boston Terrier

Congrats! You've successfully navigated the world of socialization and training, and now we're onto the next key topic - nutrition and exercise. Yes, we're transitioning from 'My Fair Lady' to 'Rocky.' Just imagine a miniature Sylvester Stallone, but cuter and with a sleeker coat. In this chapter, we will cover all the important aspects of your Boston Terrier's diet, exercise regimen, and overall well-being. Think of it as personal training and meal planning, but instead of protein shakes and dumbbells, you get kibble and tennis balls. Brace yourself, things are about to get tasty and energetic!

Proper Nutrition for a Healthy Dog

You know the saying, "You are what you eat?" Well, that goes for your Boston Terrier too. No, your dog won't turn into a kibble or a bone, but what they consume can have a major impact on their overall health. You wouldn't want to feast on junk food daily (I mean, we've all had that dream, but reality calls), and neither should your little canine buddy.

Let's start with the basics: food. Kibble, wet food, raw, cooked - there are more options on the dog food market than flavors at a gelato stand in Rome. To make things even more complicated, every brand has their "complete and balanced" formula. So how do you navigate this culinary labyrinth? Well, let's break it down.

First off, kibble. It's like the cereal of the dog world – convenient, long-lasting, and available in different flavors. But just like cereal, not all kibble is created equal. Look for brands that have a high-quality protein source, like chicken, beef, or fish, listed as the first ingredient. This means protein is the primary component of the food. Try to avoid brands with too many fillers such as corn and wheat, or unpronounceable ingredients that sound more like a science project than a meal.

Now, onto wet food. Imagine a candlelit dinner with a juicy steak – that's what wet food is for dogs. It's usually more flavorful and palatable than kibble, and it provides additional hydration. It can be an excellent option for picky eaters, but be cautious – too much wet food can lead to weight gain and dental issues.

Have you ever seen those 'gourmet' dog foods, where you can see the pieces of vegetables and meat? That's what we call fresh, cooked food. It's made with whole ingredients and looks like something you'd serve at your dinner table. Many dogs find this option appetizing, and it can be healthier, given that it's typically lower in processed ingredients. However, it's often pricier than other options and has a shorter shelf-life.

The last contender in our lineup is raw food. This diet is supposed to mimic what dogs would eat in the wild – raw meat, bones, fruits, and vegetables. Some swear by it, claiming it gives their dogs shinier coats, cleaner teeth, and more energy. But it's not without controversy, as it may pose risks of bacterial contamination and may not be nutritionally complete.

Remember, your Boston Terrier's diet will depend on their age, size, health, and activity level. For example, puppies need more calories since they're growing (and to fuel those adorable playtimes). Adult dogs, especially those who have been neutered or spayed, need fewer calories to avoid weight gain.

Treats are the icing on the cake of your Boston Terrier's diet. They're great for training and bonding, but they can also pack a caloric punch. Make sure treats don't make up more than 10% of your pup's daily caloric intake. Also, aim for healthy treats. Think of them as the dog version of a fruit snack—yummy but still good for them.

Lastly, keep in mind that changes to a dog's diet should be done gradually to prevent digestive upset. So, no matter which type of food you choose, introduce it slowly. Oh, and don't forget the water! Hydration is a vital part of your Boston Terrier's health, so always ensure they have fresh water available.

Nutrition can feel like a tricky subject, but once you get the hang of it, it's as easy as pie. Healthy pie, of course! Remember, a well-fed Boston Terrier.

The Role of Exercise in Your Boston Terrier's Life

Picture this: Your Boston Terrier, dressed in a mini sweatband and neon leggings, doing doggie push-ups and squats. While this might not be exactly how exercise looks for your pup, it's important to remember that physical activity is as important for them as it is for us humans (minus the neon leggings, perhaps).

You see, Boston Terriers are a vivacious and energetic breed. Like a tiny, fur-covered ball of energy, ready to bounce around at the slightest provocation. Exercise isn't just about burning off this energy (although it's a big part) – it's also a crucial part of their physical and mental health.

Let's kick things off by talking about the physical benefits. Regular exercise helps maintain a healthy weight. Much like us, if dogs consume more calories than they burn, they gain weight. And, while a pudgy pooch might be cute to look at, overweight dogs can suffer from a host of health issues, from heart disease to arthritis.

Exercise also keeps your Boston Terrier's joints flexible and muscles strong. It's like taking your dog to the gym, but instead of lifting weights, they're playing fetch or running around the park. It's a fun way to stay in shape – maybe we humans could learn a thing or two from our furry friends!

But the benefits of exercise don't stop at physical health. It's a mental game, too. Physical activity provides an outlet for your dog's natural instincts – running, chasing, fetching, exploring. This mental stimulation can prevent boredom and associated behavioral issues like chewing on your favorite shoes or redecorating your living room with toilet paper.

Now, you might be wondering: How much exercise does my Boston Terrier need? Well, as energetic as they are, Boston Terriers aren't marathon runners. Usually, a couple of short to moderate walks per day, combined with some playtime, will keep them happy and healthy.

This brings us to the 'what' of exercising your Boston Terrier. Variety is the spice of life, and this goes for your pup's exercise routine too! Mixing things up keeps exercise fun and engaging. One day you could go for a walk, another day play fetch, and another day set up a mini agility course in your backyard or living room.

Remember, exercise isn't just a 'chore' to check off your list. It's a bonding opportunity! It's a time to connect with your furry best friend – and maybe show off their expertly executed fetch skills to the neighborhood.

As with all things, it's important to be mindful of your Boston Terrier's individual needs and limits. Older dogs or those with health issues may not be able to exercise as much. Always consult with your vet to tailor an exercise routine that suits your pup.

And don't forget, hydration is key! Always bring water for your Boston Terrier during exercise, especially in warm weather.

In the end, remember that exercise is an essential piece of the pet care puzzle. A well-exercised Boston Terrier is a happy, healthy Boston Terrier. Plus, who can resist the sight of a content, panting pup, ready for a nap after a good workout? So, lace up your walking shoes, grab a frisbee, and let your Boston Terrier show you how exercise is truly done.

Chapter 7: Dealing with Behavioral Issues

Just as your Boston Terrier will master tricks like a boss, they might also pick up a few less-than-adorable habits. But worry not! Behavioral issues, while frustrating, are usually just a side effect of a confused pup trying to navigate the human world. In this chapter, we'll turn your pup from Boston Terror to Boston Terrier. So, buckle up for a wild ride through the landscape of doggy behavioral issues, packed with tips, tricks, and maybe even a few dog puns. Let's navigate the hurdles together, one paw-step at a time!

Common Behavioral Problems in Boston Terriers

Alrighty then! Let's delve into the fascinating, occasionally exasperating, world of Boston Terrier behavior. Each dog breed has its own unique characteristics and Boston Terriers are no exception. Being knowledgeable about these will make your life as a Boston parent smoother than a freshly groomed pooch.

First up, the "separation anxiety". This is as real as your obsession with reality TV. Terriers are social butterflies, just like you at a summer barbecue! They thrive on human companionship and could get a tad bit upset when left alone. You may come home to chewed furniture, or a harmonious canine opera echoing through your house. It's their way of saying, "I missed you!"

Second, Boston Terriers can be a little, well, 'terrier-torial'. You see, these guys have a bit of Napoleon complex going on. Small in size, large in spirit! They can sometimes get possessive over their toys or food. But hey, who among us hasn't felt a primal urge to protect our last slice of pizza?

Third, we've got the "jumping joy" syndrome. Boston Terriers are as jubilant as a kid in a candy store, and they express this by jumping up on people. It's their way of saying, "Hello, love me!" But guests might not appreciate a pooch bounding up at them, even if he is as cute as a button.

Next, the "barking brigade". Some Boston Terriers could give an opera singer a run for their money. If your Boston is barking excessively, it's essential to find the root cause.

Are they bored? Anxious? Or did they just see a squirrel? Oh, the horror!

And then, there's the 'digging drama'. If you notice your garden looking like a tiny meteor shower just hit it, it's probably your Boston Terrier's masterpiece. For them, digging is like a high-intensity sport and the yard is their playground.

Remember, though, that each Boston Terrier is unique. Some may exhibit these behaviors, while others might be as angelic as the pictures suggest. Understanding these common tendencies, though, is like getting a cheat sheet for Boston Terrier parenthood.

The key to handling these issues is patience, understanding, and a little bit of humor. Think about it - the best comedies have a hint of drama, right? And, well, behavioral problems in Boston Terriers provide you with both in ample measure!

Now, take a deep breath. It's all part of the journey. After all, our little quirks are what make us interesting, right? And who could resist the charm of a Boston Terrier, even when they're making their best attempt to transform your yard into the surface of the moon. All in a day's work for these lovable little rascals!

Remember, when it comes to the highs and lows of Boston Terrier behavior, understanding and patience go a long way. After all, nobody's perfect - even if your Boston Terrier comes pretty close. Well, except for the garden, of course. That could definitely use some work.

Strategies for Correcting Bad Habits

So you've become familiar with the quirks of your Boston Terrier. You're probably thinking, "What now?" Let's dive right into the fabulous world of modifying dog behavior, because let's face it, a perfectly behaved Boston Terrier is like a unicorn - beautiful, magical, and not really existing.

But, chin up, sunshine! You've got this. Let's take it one issue at a time. For our friends with separation anxiety, the first step is to make your departures and arrivals low-key. No need for a grand opera of goodbyes or a ticker-tape parade when you get back. They'll get the message: your leaving is no biggie!

Next up, the "terrier-torial" issue. For our little Napoleons, teaching them the "leave it" or "drop it" commands is like giving them their personal Rosetta Stone for the human world. This might require a few treats and patience, but remember, nobody became a multilinguist overnight!

Now let's tackle the overexcited jumper. Picture this: you're coming home from work, and your Boston Terrier treats you like you've been away for years (or at least a few hours). You can discourage this by ignoring them when they jump and giving them attention when all paws are on the ground. It's like playing a canine version of 'Simon says'.

For the vocal virtuosos among our Boston Terriers, the trick is to figure out why they're sounding the alarm. If it's boredom, a new chew toy might do the trick. If it's anxiety, try to remove the stressor. Remember, every bark is a sentence in 'Boston Terrier' language. It's up to you to translate!

The digging, oh the digging. If your garden has started resembling a lunar landscape, it's time to act. Provide a designated 'digging zone' - maybe a sandbox - and when they start excavating elsewhere, redirect them to the approved site. It's like giving them their own little construction project, minus the neon vests and hard hats.

Now, let's get one thing straight. You're not going to see changes overnight. Like a fine wine or that cheese you forgot at the back of the fridge, good things take time. And yes, there might be moments when you're considering buying stock in furniture because your Boston Terrier's teething or trading your manicured lawn for a dirt pit. But hang in there, help is on the way!

Training your Boston Terrier is about consistency, repetition, and rewards. It's like teaching them a choreographed dance routine. They need to learn the steps (commands), practice them until they're perfect, and get a standing ovation (treats) when they do it right.

Remember, the goal isn't to make your Boston Terrier into an emotionless robot-dog, but to manage their behavior so you both live harmoniously. The 'bad' behaviors are often just them trying to communicate or fulfill a need. So, keep your sense of humor, be patient, and know that every day is a new opportunity to learn and grow together.

Lastly, don't forget to celebrate your victories, no matter how small they seem. Did your Boston Terrier finally drop the chewed-up slipper when you said "drop it"? That's awesome! Throw a little party. After all, who needs an excuse for more treats? So, fellow Boston Terrier comrades, on to the battlegrounds of behavior modification! It's a wild ride, but trust me, it's worth it.

Chapter 8: The Aging Boston Terrier

So you've weathered the puppy storms, navigated the teenage years, and now you're sailing into the sunset of your Boston Terrier's golden years. It's like entering a new realm where the toys gather dust a bit longer and the snores from your couch companion are a bit louder. But don't despair, my friend, because aging, like a fine artisanal cheese, brings its own rich depth to the bond between you and your furry companion. This chapter is your guide to understanding, caring for, and savoring every moment of these tender years with your Boston Terrier, because a slower pace doesn't mean less adventure; it's just set to a different soundtrack.

Special Considerations for Senior Dogs

If you think senior Boston Terriers are just younger pups with a bit more grey around the snout, buckle up, buttercup, because we're about to delve into the mysterious world of canine geriatrics. Let's get real - there's more to a Boston Terrier's golden years than a transition to 'senior' labeled kibble and the occasional bout of forgetfulness about where they buried their favorite toy.

First things first, we need to talk about that physique. No, we're not body shaming our senior Boston Terriers; we love their rolls as much as we love our own. But as our adorable buddies age, their metabolism can slow down, just like ours. It's not a conspiracy between you and your Boston Terrier against the world; it's just nature. So, we need to be vigilant about diet and portion control. Exercise remains essential too, but remember, we're now jogging through the park, not sprinting like we're being chased by a horde of squirrels.

Did you know that a Boston Terrier's teeth are just as prone to aging as the rest of their body? Their dazzling doggy smile can dull over the years, with dental problems becoming more common. Regular cleaning at home and routine dental check-ups are key here. Don't fret, though. Imagine tooth brushing time as just another bonding moment that ends with minty fresh doggy kisses!

Aging can bring a set of new sensory challenges. Eyesight might fade, and hearing may lessen, but your bond with your Boston Terrier can grow stronger. Remember, patience is key. The phrase "you can't teach an old dog new tricks" was clearly not coined by a Boston Terrier owner. Older Bostons can adapt, but it takes time and kindness. Hand signals, scent trails, night lights, there are lots of ways to help your fuzzy buddy navigate their changing world.

Just like with us humans, old age may also mean that the immune system isn't quite the powerhouse it used to be. Regular check-ups at the vet are crucial. There are illnesses that are more prevalent in senior dogs, and early detection is a game-changer. Don't worry, though, we're not turning our homes into canine hospitals, but we are turning ourselves into observant, proactive pet parents.

While health is paramount, let's not forget about the joy. Senior Boston Terriers might not have the boundless energy of their puppy selves, but they still crave fun. They're like grandparents who can still bust a move at a wedding; you just have to pick the right song. Short walks, gentle games, and lots of cuddles will keep their tails wagging.

Lastly, it's crucial to remember that the aging process is as unique as your Boston Terrier's personality. There isn't a one-size-fits-all guidebook to this new stage of life, but that's okay. You and your Boston Terrier are explorers in this land of senior pet ownership.

Growing older with your Boston Terrier is a privilege. It's an opportunity to deepen your bond, to slow down, and to savor the sweet, simple moments. So here's to the slow walks, the long naps, the gentle playtimes, and to the love that only deepens with time. Here's to the golden years! After all, gold is precious, isn't it?

Adjusting Training Techniques for Older Dogs

Alright, people, it's time to put on our doggy training caps – but make them slightly softer, a bit bigger, and definitely more patient. Yes, we're talking about adjusting training techniques for your older Boston Terrier. Remember, age is just a number; it might be a higher number than before, but it's just a number nevertheless!

First off, we need to embrace patience. Imagine if you had to learn quantum physics in a foreign language – that's how your Boston Terrier might feel learning new tricks or unlearning old habits. So take a deep breath, sip your kombucha, and remember: it's not a race. As the great philosopher of our time, never said, "In the dog world, patience is more than a virtue; it's a necessity."

Next, consistency is key. If "Sit" meant "Put your adorable furry bottom on the floor" yesterday, today, and tomorrow, it must mean the same thing next week, too. Consistent commands, coupled with consistent rewards, help keep your Boston Terrier on track. And remember, the reward doesn't always have to be a treat – sometimes a simple "Good job, buddy!" can make their tail waggle with joy.

Speaking of rewards, positive reinforcement is your best friend – and not just because it makes you feel like Oprah giving away cars on her show. Positive reinforcement helps older dogs associate the new behavior with happy feelings. It's like when you finally remember to bring your reusable shopping bags and treat yourself to an extra cookie. That cookie makes the memory stick!

Sometimes, though, new tricks can be, well, tricky. If you're finding a particular command challenging, try breaking it down into smaller steps. This is what dog trainers refer to as "shaping." It's like learning to bake by starting with boxed brownies before moving on to soufflés.

Don't forget to keep training sessions short and sweet. As dogs age, their attention span and stamina might dwindle a bit. Imagine if you had to sit through a 3-hour lecture about soil composition; you'd want a nap after 15 minutes too!

Additionally, consider incorporating training into your everyday routine. Ask your Boston Terrier to sit before meals, to stay when you open the door, or to come when you're getting ready for a walk. It's a low-pressure way to reinforce their training, and it helps keep their minds sharp.

Of course, we need to consider the physical abilities of our senior pooches. If jumping was a bit hard on your Boston Terrier's joints as a spry young thing, it's likely a no-go in their senior years. Opt for commands and tricks that are gentle on their bodies.

If you've had your Boston Terrier since they were a puppy, remember that senior dog training is not about changing who they are. It's about adjusting to their current stage of life. Like how you'd trade your college ramen for a quinoa salad, or how you'd swap an all-nighter for a solid 8 hours of sleep.

Finally, celebrate your victories, both big and small. Every step in the right direction is a cause for celebration. Your Boston Terrier wants to make you happy, so let them know when they do. Love, after all, is the secret ingredient in every successful dog training endeavor.

Adjusting training techniques for an older Boston Terrier might seem daunting at first, but remember: you're not alone. You have your Boston Terrier, who loves you more than they love chasing squirrels or digging up your garden. You're a team, through thick and thin, through puppyhood and into these golden years. So hold onto your patience, fill your pockets with treats, and step into this new adventure with the confidence of a dog chasing a Frisbee on a sunny day!

The Boston Sniffles

Okay, let's talk about that classic Boston Terrier symphony - the snuffles, the snores, the Darth Vader impressions in the middle of the night. They may be music to our ears, but sometimes they signal something a bit more serious.

Firstly, it's important to understand that the charming smushed face of your Boston Terrier, while absolutely adorbs, comes with a fancy term - brachycephalic. That's just a ten-dollar word for "short-nosed." This squished snoot can sometimes lead to breathing issues, which in turn can lead to those snores that can outshine a foghorn.

Now, don't rush to the vet in a panic just yet. Snoring doesn't always mean trouble. Sometimes, it just means your Boston Terrier found an extra comfy, extra snore-inducing position on their favorite pillow (or, let's be real, your favorite pillow). But other times, it can be a sign of something called Brachycephalic Syndrome. It's a big name, but think of it as your dog's version of snoring so loud you can't sleep...but all the time.

Brachycephalic Syndrome includes stenotic nares (narrow nostrils), an elongated soft palate (extra tissue blocking the throat), and everted laryngeal saccules (tissue that gets pulled into the windpipe and can cause a blockage). If your Boston is struggling to breathe, getting tired easily, or their snores sound more like gasps or chokes, it's time to consult with your vet.

When you visit the vet, they'll do a thorough exam and maybe some tests to see what's going on. And while you might wish you could teach your Boston to breathe through their butt like a sea cucumber (yes, it's a thing), the actual treatment options are a tad more traditional.

Treatment depends on what's causing the issue. If your dog's nostrils are as narrow as the last pair of jeans you tried to squeeze into, your vet might recommend surgery to widen them. It's like getting a nose job, but for breathing instead of vanity.

If the problem lies with the soft palate, your vet might suggest trimming it back. It's done under general anesthesia, and your pup will likely be back to their normal, goofy self in no time. Well, maybe with a little less snoring.

In some cases, weight can contribute to the issue. If your Boston has been indulging in too many treats, your vet may recommend a diet. And no, pizza crusts don't count as a food group, as much as your Boston tries to convince you otherwise.

Surgery might sound scary, but remember, it's about improving your dog's quality of life. Plus, veterinary surgeons have been doing these procedures for years. They've got this - and so do you.

Now, keep in mind, not every snore requires drastic measures. Some lifestyle adjustments can help. Keeping your home cool can ease your Boston's breathing. Also, using a harness instead of a collar prevents pressure on their throat, making walks a breezier affair.

And remember, the snoring that you initially thought was as charming as your Boston's expressive eyes, is just part of them. But it's always important to ensure it's not detracting from their quality of life. You're the DJ here, and it's your job to make sure the symphony plays on. You've got the conduction baton, and by golly, you're going to lead your Boston Terrier orchestra to a crescendo of happiness. Because that's what it's all about - ensuring your Boston Terrier's life is as full of joy as the love they bring to yours.

Conclusion: Your Journey Together

L ife with a Boston Terrier is like being in a rom-com: unpredictable, filled with belly laughs, and brimming with love. It's a tale where the leading stars are you and your furry friend, and every day is another scene. From puppyhood's wild antics to the mellow rhythms of their golden years, the journey will be dotted with hilarity, challenges, but most importantly, a bond that transcends species. With the wisdom from these chapters, you're now equipped to be the co-star your Boston Terrier deserves. So go forth, let the cameras roll, and enjoy every moment of this beautiful, tail-wagging journey. After all, life is better with a Boston!

Celebrating Progress and Milestones

Ah, milestones! They're not just for human kids, you know. As the proud parent of a Boston Terrier, there will be moments when you'll want to whip out your smartphone and capture that first sit, the inaugural fetch, or maybe even the initial encounter with the infamous vacuum cleaner. These are the glorious, Instagram-worthy victories that we're going to chat about. Let's pop that virtual champagne and celebrate those wins, shall we?

First things first, let's start with the 'Puppy Firsts.' Just like human babies, there are a heap of 'firsts' to look forward to with your Boston puppy. You might think, "Gosh, it's just a puppy sitting, what's the big deal?" I'll tell you what's the big deal. Your little furball has just mastered the art of tushie placement on your command. That's one small sit for your Boston, one giant leap for Boston-kind! So, go ahead and celebrate that achievement like your Boston just won the Puppy Olympics.

The first fetch is another momentous milestone. I mean, sure, your Boston didn't discover the Theory of Relativity, but retrieving that toy and bringing it back? Genius level, right there. It's the doggy version of a graduation ceremony, but instead of a diploma, your Boston would probably appreciate a treat and a belly rub.

Next up, the daunting stairs conquest. For a puppy, a flight of stairs is like a mountain range. But that moment when they brave the climb for the first time? It's an Everest moment, sans the sub-zero temperatures and lack of oxygen. Your Boston, the brave adventurer, has vanquished the intimidating staircase mountain!

Let's not forget socialization. That first successful doggy date without any drama is definitely something to remember. It's like your Boston just nailed their first job interview. Celebrate it with extra playtime or maybe a new toy. They deserve it, after all.

But wait, there's more! Your Boston Terrier will continue to hit new milestones throughout their life. They're lifelong learners, you see. They might learn a new trick or even a fun game, showing off that intelligence they're so well known for. When they do, that's your cue to cheer them on, shower them with praise, and let them know that they've just outsmarted a fox in a dog suit.

Now, as your Boston gets older, the milestones might change, but they'll still be there. Maybe it's mastering a more challenging command or learning to adjust to a new diet. Each win, no matter how small, is still a victory worth celebrating.

Remember, every dog - just like every human - has its own pace. So don't stress if your Boston hasn't nailed down a trick that the neighborhood Poodle learned in a jiffy. Keep the faith, maintain the patience, and when your Boston does achieve that milestone, party like it's 1999.

In the grand scheme of things, these milestones are much more than social media highlights or cocktail party anecdotes. They're proof of the incredible bond between you and your Boston Terrier, a testament to the trust and love that you've nurtured over time. So keep celebrating, because each victory, no matter how small, contributes to a lifetime of happiness with your Boston. Now that's what I call a paw-some journey!

So there you have it! The milestones and victories that make the dog parenting journey an exciting adventure. Remember, each step is a cause for celebration. So go ahead, throw that paw-ty, and let the kibble rain down. Just remember to take lots of pictures, because these are the moments that make life with a Boston Terrier truly special.

The Lifelong Bond Between You and Your Boston Terrier

If we rewind to the beginning of our fur-filled journey, we started with an idea: a dream of adding a small, energetic, bat-eared wonder known as a Boston Terrier to your life. You were preparing for an adventure, as thrilling as bungee jumping, and as rewarding as finding the Holy Grail - only this time, the treasure had a wet nose and a wagging tail.

Each day with your Boston Terrier, it turns out, is a new chapter in an epic novel, filled with love, joy, challenges, and lots of doggy kisses. Every sunrise brings the promise of a new escapade, every sunset a peaceful end to a day well spent. It's like living in a perpetual feel-good movie where your Boston is the undisputed star.

Life with your Boston Terrier is not just about training sessions, healthy diets, and exercise routines. It's about laughter that rings out when they do something silly, the pride that swells when they learn a new trick, the comfort when they snuggle up to you at the end of a long day. It's like having a live-in comedian, a lifetime student, a personal trainer, and a furry therapist all rolled into one.

Your bond with your Boston will grow and evolve, much like a fine wine or a timeless classic movie. One day you might realize that the little rascal who once chewed your favorite shoes is now your most loyal companion, someone who can read your moods better than any human ever could. This relationship isn't just about ownership; it's a mutual, soulful connection. It's like having a non-judgmental best friend who thinks you're the moon, the stars, and all the doggy treats in between.

There will be challenges, of course. Days when your patience is tested, nights when you worry, moments when you question your sanity. But then, your Boston will look at you with those big, expressive eyes full of unconditional love, and you'll realize that every hurdle was worth it. It's akin to mastering a difficult dance routine, only to find that the end performance is breathtaking.

Over the years, your Boston Terrier will inevitably change. They'll age, slow down, and their once black-and-white coat may be tinged with gray. But the bond between you both will never fade. In fact, it'll only grow stronger, like a tree rooted deep in the earth, weathering every storm. It's like discovering that, despite the passing years, your favorite song still makes your heart flutter.

Your Boston Terrier's loyalty will never waver. They will be there for you through thick and thin, during late-night TV binges, early morning coffee sips, jubilant celebrations, and quiet tears. They'll be your constant in a world of variables, your rock in a sea of uncertainty.

It's like having your very own superhero, just without the cape.

As you both grow older, you'll discover new facets of your relationship. You'll see your Boston in a new light, appreciate them even more, and understand that the bond you share is irreplaceable. It's like watching a stunning sunrise after a dark night, a beautiful revelation of love and companionship.

Finally, when it's time for your Boston Terrier to cross the rainbow bridge, they'll leave behind a legacy of love, lessons learned, and memories that will make you smile even on the gloomiest days. It's like having a piece of your heart living outside your body, filled with every wag, every bark, every loving glance.

So, as we conclude our journey together, remember this: The bond between you and your Boston Terrier isn't just about pet and owner. It's a profound connection, a lifelong journey filled with laughter, love, tears, and joy. It's a friendship that transcends words, a love that knows no bounds. And that, dear friend, is the true beauty of sharing your life with a Boston Terrier.

Appendix

A. Recommended Products and Resources for Boston Terrier Owners

When it comes to spoiling your Boston Terrier, the sky's the limit! There's an abundance of products out there designed to make life with your furry friend even more fabulous. Here's a roundup of must-haves that will have your Boston doing the happy dance:

- **Comfortable Harness:** Look for one that's adjustable, breathable, and doesn't put pressure on your Boston's neck. The 'Puppia Soft Dog Harness' fits the bill perfectly, and comes in an array of chic colors.

- **Engaging Toys:** Bostons love playtime! Consider a variety of toys like the 'KONG Classic Dog Toy' for mental stimulation, a 'Chuckit! Ultra Ball' for energetic fetch games, or 'Outward Hound Hide-A-Squirrel Puzzle' to challenge their clever minds.

- **Quality Dog Food:** Choose a nutrient-dense food tailored to their age, size, and health condition. Brands like 'Blue

Buffalo Life Protection Formula' offer excellent options.

- **Comfy Bed:** Bostons love their beauty sleep. Opt for a cozy bed like the 'Furhaven Pet Dog Bed', that's easy to clean and provides great support for those adorable little bodies.

- **Training Treats:** Training becomes a fun game when there are yummy rewards involved. 'Zuke's Mini Naturals' are small, low-calorie treats that are perfect for teaching new tricks.

- **Dental Care Products:** Dental health is crucial for Bostons. Consider investing in 'Greenies Original Dental Dog Treats' and a 'Petrodex Enzymatic Toothpaste for Dogs' for those pearly whites.

- **Climate-appropriate Clothing:** Given their thin coat, Bostons can get chilly quickly. Check out brands like 'Gooby Fleece Dog Vest' for warm, stylish apparel.

- **Grooming Supplies:** A grooming kit with essentials like a gentle shampoo (like 'Burt's Bees for Dogs All-Natural Shampoo'), a slicker brush, and dog-safe nail clippers will keep your Boston looking dapper.

- **Health Supplements:** Consult your vet about adding supplements like fish oil or glucosamine (like 'Nutramax Cosequin DS Plus') to your Boston's diet, especially as they age.

- **Car Seat Cover:** If your Boston is a regular co-pilot on your adventures, a durable car seat cover like the 'URPOWER Dog Seat Cover' can protect your vehicle's interiors while providing comfort for your furry friend.

As always, each Boston is unique and these recommendations may not suit every Boston Terrier out there. It's essential to observe your pet's behavior, consult with your vet, and choose the products that best meet your Boston's specific needs and preferences.

B. Glossary of Common Training Terms

- **Positive Reinforcement:** This involves giving your Boston a reward (a treat, praise, or a favorite toy) to reinforce good behavior. The idea is that the dog will repeat the good behavior to get more rewards.

- **Negative Punishment:** This isn't as harsh as it sounds! It means taking away something your dog likes (like attention) when they misbehave, to decrease the likelihood of the behavior repeating.

- **Clicker Training:** A method of positive reinforcement where a clicker is used to mark the exact moment a desired behavior occurs, followed by a reward.

- **Command:** A verbal or visual cue to get your dog to do something. For example, saying "Sit" or holding your hand flat, palm up, for 'stay'.

- **Proofing:** Testing your dog's command recall in different environments with various distractions.

- **Marker:** A signal to your dog that a reward is coming. This can be a clicker, a word like "Yes!" or "Good!", or even a short whistle.

- **Lure:** Using something your dog likes (usually a treat) to guide them into performing a specific behavior.

- **Redirect:** Changing your dog's focus from an undesired behavior to a desired one.

- **Socialization:** The process of exposing your dog to a variety of experiences, people, places, and other animals to help them be comfortable and confident in different situations.

- **Desensitization:** Gradual exposure to a stimulus that your dog is afraid of or reactive to, in order to decrease their reaction.

- **Counter-conditioning:** Changing your dog's emotional response to a stimulus. For example, if your Boston is scared of the vacuum, feeding them treats while you vacuum can help change their feelings about it.

- **Enrichment:** Activities, toys, or other additions to your dog's environment to stimulate their mind and encourage natural behaviors.

- **Behavior Modification:** Using various techniques to change a particular, established behavior in a dog.

Each of these methods is a tool in your toolbox as you work to raise a well-adjusted, happy Boston Terrier. Remember, patience and consistency are key!

About the Author

L acy Peters, a native Floridian in her mid-20s, is the epitome of a modern-day dog whisperer. As the proud pet parent to a pack of six diverse dogs, her love for these four-legged friends stretches beyond just companionship. She has transformed her adoration into a fulfilling career as a dog trainer, providing guidance and wisdom to dogs and their humans alike. Living in the

Sunshine State, where every day feels like a dog day, she cherishes the constant bustle and excitement that her furry family brings.

When she's not busy transforming lovable pups into well-behaved companions, Lacy indulges in her love for the written word. Writing is her sanctuary, her personal little corner in a world filled with wagging tails and playful barks. It's here that she crafts her experiences, insights, and love for canines into helpful guides for other dog lovers. Despite her accomplishments and the popularity of her work, Lacy prefers to live life away from the glaring lights of social media, cherishing her privacy and the simple pleasures of life.

Outside of her professional realm, Lacy is just like any other twenty-something woman who loves the beach, good food, and engrossing movies. She often spends her free time with her supportive boyfriend, whether it's having dinner at their favorite local spot, catching the latest blockbuster, or simply strolling along the stunning Florida coastline with their six furry friends trailing along. Her life may be private, but it's brimming with love, laughter, and of course, an endless supply of doggie cuddles. Lacy Peters, through her books and life, exemplifies that living a quiet life doesn't mean a lack of adventure - especially when you share it with dogs.

Made in the USA
Las Vegas, NV
22 October 2024

10321826R00069